THE IMPORTANCE
OF THE BIBLE

William Neil

DENHOLM HOUSE PRESS

Robert Denholm House, Nutfield,
Surrey RH1 4HW

First published 1975

© Denholm House Press

ISBN 0 85213 111 9

*This edition is not to be sold in
Australia or New Zealand*

Cover design: Anne Farncombe
Illustrations: June Brown

Printed in Hungary

EDITORIAL FOREWORD

Great convictions are basic to our Christian faith. Most Christians know something about them but would welcome—and often ask for—help in coming to a greater knowledge of them.

This series of books examines these convictions one by one and tries to state, clearly and definitely, widely accepted Christian belief.

Each writer has, of course, his own viewpoint and has not been expected to conceal this. But we think the conclusions reached fairly represent what a very great company of Christians believe and build their lives upon.

The books are suitable for individual reading or for use in groups. Questions for discussion are not included since we feel these are best drawn up by group leaders who can tailor them to the particular needs of their own groups.

The Bible references are an important part of the books and should be looked up and carefully considered.

THE BIBLE REFERENCES
in this book are to the New English Bible

The Importance of the Bible...

There is no other book like the Bible in the whole world. Something approaching fifty million copies of it, or parts of it, are sold or distributed every year in all five continents, translated into almost every known language and dialect. This is twice as many copies as were sold or distributed a mere fifteen years ago so there can be no doubt about the Bible's popularity. When we remember that the average sales of a novel in this country are altogether about three thousand we can see that this Bible is in a class by itself. When Sir Walter Scott was dying he asked his son-in-law and biographer, John Gibson Lockhart, to read to him. Looking round Scott's vast library at Abbotsford Lockhart asked him which book he wanted him to read. Scott replied: "Need you ask? There is but one."

Of course all the great world religions have their own sacred books. Muslims have the Koran, Hindus have the Upanishads, Jews and Christians share the same book, the Old Testament, to which Christians add the New Testament as its sequel and completion. This is because for Christians, the New Testament, which tells us all we know about Jesus and the beginning of the Church which he founded, is not only the climax of the story which the Bible tells but also the record of the most significant events in the whole of human history. This is a tremendous claim to make, but it is a claim on which every Christian must be prepared to stake his life.

All religions worship the same God, although they may speak and think of him in different ways. Christians believe that God has disclosed something of the mystery of his Being and of his purpose for the world to saints and sages in all religions, but that it is only through Jesus that he has revealed the whole truth about himself and about ourselves, showing us what sort of people we really are, what God wants us to become, how we should live with one another and what sort of society we should be aiming to build. Nobody in his senses would imagine that the Bible gives detailed answers to all these complicated questions, but it does give us signposts pointing us in the right direction.

ONE BOOK IN TWO PARTS

Now although we feel rightly that the New Testament is for Christians the crucial part of the Bible, we must never forget that the Bible is one book and not two. Old Testament and New Testament are not only bound within the same covers, they are both dependent on each other and we cannot understand the second part without the first. A Chinese pastor said that "reading the Old Testament is like eating crab. It turns out to be mostly shell with very little meat in it." In some ways this is true and we shall have to come back to this point later. But what we

6

must not forget is that Jesus was a Jew, brought up to know and love the Old Testament, and that what he teaches us about God and ourselves is based on what he himself had been taught by the rabbis in the village school in Nazareth, and what he had heard in the local synagogue. Of course Jesus thought things out for himself and did not simply hand on to his followers what he had been taught. He was highly critical of some features of Jewish religion and wanted to change many of them. But the faith of the psalmists and prophets of the Old Testament was the faith of Jesus too, and he passed it on to his first disciples, who made it the foundation of Christian belief.

Yet though we say that the Bible is one book divided into two parts, it only needs a casual glance to see that the two parts are in many ways quite different. Obviously the New Testament is very much smaller than the Old Testament, about a third of its size. But the two parts of the Bible are also different in character. The Old Testament is a varied collection of history, poetry, philosophy, fiction, biography, autobiography, proverbs and prophecy. The New Testament has much less variety. There are four short sketches of the life of Jesus, a brief account of the first thirty years of the story of the Church, and the rest is mostly letters to one or other Christian community from one or other missionary leader, principally St. Paul. Why is there this difference?

THE OLD TESTAMENT

According to an old legend when churchmen could not agree on what books should be included in the Bible and what should be left out, the books were spread on the floor in front of the altar, prayers were said, and then those books that were meant to be included hopped up on to the altar and the rejects remained quietly where they were. Needless to say things did not happen that way, nor did the Bible come down from the sky all neatly wrapped up and tied with paper and string.

The Old Testament is the sacred writings of the Jewish people, built up and collected over a period of a thousand years. It started like any other literature with folk songs, ballads and camp-fire stories of heroes and battles. In time these were put into writing, and gradually over the centuries various other items were added—laws for the good government of the people, hymns for public and private worship, records of kings and statesmen, sermons preached by the prophets of Israel, guidance for the good life from the wise men in the community.

This process of building up an authoritative holy book for the Jewish people was not completed until after the coming of Christ, and the Jews took copies with them wherever they went as they were scattered to the four corners of the known world when their country and its capital Jerusalem were devastated by the Romans in A.D. 70. Although they had no longer a land of their own they had in their holy book the record of God's dealings with them in the past, and his promise that he would be with them wherever they went.

THE NEW TESTAMENT

The New Testament was built up in a much shorter time, not a thousand years but more like a hundred. It came into being as a direct result of the impact of Jesus upon a handful of Jews who became convinced that this was not just another prophet like Isaiah or Jeremiah, whose teaching was handed down in their scriptures, but someone quite unique, who spoke as no other Jew had ever spoken and who had done things that no other Jew had done. Above all they felt that through him they had come to know God in a radically new and intimate way, and that their lives had been transformed through their encounter with Jesus. This was something they could not keep to themselves, and so they went out to proclaim to their Jewish countrymen and then later to the wider world what Jesus had done for them.

They told the story of what Jesus had said, of how he had healed the sick, made blind men see and lame men walk, of how he had brought dead men back to life, and above all how he had himself conquered death, and was now alive and present with his followers wherever they might be. So some of them wrote all this down in what we now call the Gospels —which just means Good News—and others, such as St. Paul, wrote letters to groups of Christians up and down the Mediterranean world, encouraging, advising and strengthening them in their faith. So in a fairly short time these writings were collected to form what we know as the New Testament; which was virtually complete by A.D. 100.

THE BIBLE TODAY

So far we have been looking at how the Bible came into existence. But before we go any further there is one major question that must be answered. We are living in the twentieth century, in the space age, the age of electronics, of automation and the computer. Men can fly round the world in less time than it used to take to load up a donkey and travel from Nazareth to Jerusalem. We can talk in London to someone living in Calcutta. We can watch on television by satellite men walking on the moon. Electricity turns night into day and tractors and bulldozers do in a few hours what used to take men weeks of back-breaking work.

Yet when we open the Bible we find we are back in a world of oil lamps, spinning wheels and ox-drawn carts. People live in tents and not in multi-story flats. They draw their water from the village well and buy the food they cannot grow for themselves from roadside stalls and not from flashy supermarkets. Of course this way of life is still familiar to millions of villagers in Africa and Asia, but it is not surprising if people brought up in modern cities—in eastern as well as western countries—wonder how a book which springs from such a primitive background and deals with people who knew nothing of technology and the rush of present day life can have anything to say to us today.

But if we rule out the Bible on these grounds we

Then and now

must also rule out anything that was written before the twentieth century—not only the wisdom of the ancient religions of the east, apart from Christianity, but also the civilisations of Greece and Rome, to say nothing of Dante, Shakespeare, Goethe and the poets and novelists of the Victorian age in Europe and America. The truth is that all the inventions and gadgets that we have come to accept as part of our normal way of life have not made any difference to the problems that modern man has to face as acutely as the men of ancient times.

Like the people in the Bible we still have to learn how to grow up, to get on with our neighbours, to live with our families. We still get married and have to bring up our children, learn to make ends meet, cope with accidents and misfortunes, face up to illness and death, and try to keep our feet in a bewildering and changing world. These are precisely the problems with which the Bible deals for it is primarily a book about life and how we can get the most out of it. Jesus claimed that he had come "that men may have life, and may have it in all its fullness" (John 10: 10)—not an easy life or a carefree life but a full life. As we shall see, Jesus tells us that getting the most out of life depends on putting the most we can into it. But the thing we should notice at this point is that a full life in the sense that Jesus meant it does not depend on cars, fridges, TV or expensive holidays abroad. The full life in the Christian sense is an inward thing, depending on our relation to God and to other people, and it can as readily be lived in an African village as in Manhattan—probably more so.

But there is one big question that bothers a lot of young—and older—people today in a way that it did not bother our grandfathers. Science has taught us that the earth on which we live is not the centre of the universe, as people used to think, but a tiny speck in limitless space, which is full of far more and far bigger planets, constellations and galaxies than we can see with the naked eye or even a powerful telescope. When we look up into the sky on a clear night and see a host of twinkling stars we are seeing just the fringe of unknown worlds that lie beyond us. Some of them may have life on them of quite a different kind from our own. We do not yet know, but no doubt one day the scientists will be able to tell us.

Science has also taught us how to control the forces of nature in a way that our forefathers would not have thought possible. I remember an early Communist film which showed Russian peasants in a time of drought being encouraged by the local priest to pray to God to send rain—which of course did not come. Then along came the Communist technicians with tractors and bulldozers, harnessing the nearby river, building a dam, teaching the peasants that it was not prayers that were needed but irrigation, and the fields were soon burgeoning with flourishing crops. The scornful peasants were then shown chasing away their ignorant priest with his prayer-book, and worshipping progress in the shape of a tractor instead of a useless Cross upon the altar. So much has been done by science to improve the lot of mankind that it is not surprising that God seems to be more and more edged out of the picture. Do we need any more the kind of God the Bible describes who gives or withholds the rain, causing droughts and famine, and bringing them to an end when the proper prayers are said or when people mend their ways? Surely modern science can control these things much more efficiently.

Then there is the question of the Creation. The Bible seems to be saying that it all took place in a period of six days, including sun, moon, stars and the whole of the animal kingdom including man. Yet science has shown beyond a shadow of doubt that it must have taken millions of years for life to evolve on our planet, and that man comes at the end of an incredibly complex process of development from primitive organisms to the human species. Until quite recently church people could always comfort themselves by saying: "Well at least the scientists cannot create life. That is the sole prerogative of God." But is this so? It looks very much as if, to judge from recent experiments, the day will not be far off when science can do this too, and once it is established that even the most elementary form of living organism can be created it is not likely that the scientists will stop there. What kind of creatures they will produce is another story, and this may be a new problem for a future generation.

Any schoolboy knows that serpents and donkeys do not talk (Genesis 3: 1 ff; Numbers 22: 22 ff), that Moses could not have waved his magic wand and divided the Red Sea (Exodus 14: 15ff.), that Elijah could not have gone up to heaven in a chariot of fire (2 Kings 2: 11) and that Elisha could not have made an axe-head float (2 Kings 6: 6). Yet the Bible seems to be asking us to believe that unscientific things of this sort actually happened, to say nothing of Jonah's fantastic journey in a whale's belly (Jonah 1–2). Unless we are going to put the Bible on the same level as fairy-tales like Jack and the Beanstalk we must be quite clear that the last thing the Bible claims to be is a scientific textbook. We do not expect poets to write about quadratic equations or mathematicians to express their formulae in blank verse.

Truth can be expressed in many ways. Science deals with one aspect of truth, religion with another. While the scientist is concerned with how things happen, as for example, in the theory of the evolution of the universe, the Bible is concerned with the question of why there should be a universe at all. The scientist can tell us all about the mixture of chemicals that go to make up a human being, the Bible concentrates on man as a mixture of hopes and fears, passions and aspirations. There is thus no conflict between what the scientists say and what the writers of the Bible say. They are looking at things from different angles. We have been brought up in an age of science to ask such questions as: Did this really happen?—as for example in the story of God making tunics of skins for Adam and Eve (Gen. 3: 21). An ancient Hebrew reading that story would never have dreamt of asking himself if it had ever happened; he would have said to himself: What is the point of that story, what is it trying to say to me?

This meant that the writers of the Bible—particularly of the Old Testament—were far more free to use ancient tales and folk-lore to convey their message than modern writers today. They could use poetry, myths and legends which are not in our sense scientifically true, but religiously true—that is, they point to some truth about God or ourselves or the world we live in. Now it is important to remember that the writers of the earlier part of the Old Testament, which is where most of these problems arise, were not simple shepherds and farmers who believed, for example, that the first woman was made out of the rib of the first man (Genesis 2: 21–25). Stories like these were used by scholarly priests and chroniclers only a few hundred years before Christ, by which time Israel was a highly civilised and sophisticated community. But these writers knew that a vivid piece of ancient folk-lore like the story of Adam's rib could convey the man-woman relationship and the basis for marriage far more successfully than many pages of technical jargon in a medical or psychological textbook.

They not only used bits of folk-lore of this kind but found also in some of the myths of the ancient Near East—like the story of Noah's Ark (Genesis 6–9)—ways of conveying religious truth. The biblical Flood is the symbol of God's timeless judgement on the corruption of the world—in the twentieth century as much as in olden times, just as the rainbow is the symbol of his mercy, and Noah himself stands for the good man in any generation who lives by the light of conscience and who makes humanity as a whole worth preserving. In the case of all these old tales we have to look not for factual scientific truth but religious truth, truth about life.

Similarly the biblical writers used legends about holy men, as the Christian religion and indeed all religions have done, not to stretch our credulity but to convey the sense that these were indeed remarkable men who made such an impression on their times that things were said to have happened to them that do not happen to ordinary humdrum mortals. So we are told that Elijah was fed night and morning by ravens (1 Kings 17: 6), just as St. Francis was said to have stopped a river flowing past his cell at Assisi because it disturbed his prayers. We might note in passing that the story of Jonah in the whale's belly is neither myth nor legend, but a piece of pure fiction in which one marvel follows hard on the heels of another. The story was obviously meant to make people laugh, like Jesus' picture of a camel struggling to get through the eye of a needle (Matthew 19: 24), but as they laughed they would see that the author of the little tale of Jonah was teaching them a profoundly serious lesson about the love of God, contrasted with the harsh intolerance of a prophet who hated foreigners.

IS THE OLD TESTAMENT RELIABLE?

But at this point I can hear someone asking: "If the Bible is not scientifically accurate, and if it makes use of myths and legends to convey its message, can we rely on it at all as a record of things that actually happened or is it all a concoction of fantasies?" So let us try to clear this up by looking at the Old and New Testaments separately, and bring in the archaeologists to help us. And here it is important to remember what archaeology can do and what it cannot do. It can tell us that there was an ancient city state in Mesopotamia called Ur of the Chaldees (Genesis 11: 28), but it does not tell us why Abraham's father, Terah, left it or indeed if there was ever a man called Abraham living there at all. It can tell us plenty about the pharaohs of Egypt and their subject peoples. But it does not tell us anything about a small group of Hebrews who escaped from Egypt in dramatic circumstances under the leadership of Moses, which for the biblical writers was the most significant event in their whole history.

Archaeology does, however, confirm in a general way the story that the Old Testament tells of a small nation on the Mediterranean seaboard called Israel which developed into a prosperous kingdom, but which proved no match for the more powerful empires of Assyria and Babylon, and was finally eliminated as a political power by Nebuchadnezzar of Babylon in 587 B.C. At many points there are references in Mesopotamian inscriptions to historical events which the Bible also records, and archaeologists tell us that the background details of customs and legal practices in patriarchal times are accurate and trustworthy. Early this century Sir Leonard Woolley was excavating the royal graves at Ur of the Chaldees. He had dug through layers of rubble, each layer indicating evidence of a buried city, since the practice was to build a new city on the site of an older one which had been destroyed by fire or

Tablets giving the Assyrian story of Creation

invasion. At the foot of the pit where the diggers were at work, they came across pure clay which seemed to indicate that nothing further could lie beneath. Woolley had however a hunch to dig further, and sure enough the clay turned out to be merely eight feet deep and below it lay more layers of rubble indicating that the area had been inundated —perhaps by a tidal wave from the top of the Persian Gulf—and had been under water for some considerable time. Woolley sent a dramatic telegram to London: 'We have found the Flood!' And indeed this was proof that somewhere about 4000 B.C. there had been a great flood in that part of the world which gave rise to the biblical story. There is of course no archaeological evidence for the existence of the Ark, although from time to time unconfirmed reports come through of its skeleton having been spotted from the air, lying on the top of Mt. Ararat. To hold all the animals described in the story, however, the Ark would have had to be the size of the Isle of Wight!

Archaeology can therefore give us limited confirmation of the broad outline of Israel's history. The great prophets, from Isaiah to Malachi, whose utterances are preserved in the Old Testament, are also witnesses to the events of their times, and contemporary witnesses at that. We can rely on the picture they give us of the problems that faced their society, the portraits they paint of their kings and statesmen, and the fortunes and misfortunes of the ordinary people of their day, to which class most of the prophets themselves belonged. In the case of the earlier stories of the Old Testament, from Abraham onwards, we can rely on the general course of events being more or less accurately recorded, but it would be too much to expect that conversations which would be handed down by word of mouth for several centuries before being written down could be reliably reported. On the other hand ancient oriental story tellers' memories were far better than our own, and people liked to have the same story told in the same way and challenged the story-teller if he told something different. It would be like a modern child being told the story of Little Red Riding Hood and being outraged if someone were to change it so that grandma ate the wolf instead of the other way round. In those early days there were also no distractions like newspapers and television, so that people paid more attention to the spoken word.

IS THE NEW TESTAMENT RELIABLE?

A boy in a Youth Club said to me once when we were talking about this question of the reliability of the Bible: "Surely if we can believe that Jesus rose from the dead we can believe the lot, even Jonah being swallowed by the whale". This was muddled thinking. The two things are quite different. First of all, as we have already seen, the Old Testament is the literature of a nation built up over a period of a thousand years. The New Testament is the legacy of a religious community written down over a few decades, and while the events it records were still fresh in the minds of the writers. Secondly, again as we have seen, when we are reading about Jonah we are reading a piece of fiction. When we are reading about Jesus we are being told not only of a historical person, but of a person whom the writers about him believed to be like no one else who had ever lived. If Jesus was anything like what the New Testament writers say about him—and indeed what the Church has always acclaimed him to be—we must expect to find him saying things that no ordinary man would say and doing things that no ordinary man would do.

The earliest of the Gospels, Mark, dates from about 35 years after the Crucifixion. At that time there were still plenty of people about who could have challenged the facts recorded if they had been untrue. It is no greater length of time than that between the Battle of Britain and the present day. Moreover as we learn from the New Testament itself, Christian missionaries started their preaching campaigns at Pentecost (Acts 2), a few weeks after the Crucifixion, and in their preaching they included incidents in Jesus' life and many of his sayings. Again because of Jewish teaching methods, which meant largely memorising and repeating until pupils had the lessons off by heart, we may take it that the missionaries who were sent out handed on faithfully to their audiences what they themselves had been taught. It may be that they were equipped with leaflets containing collections of sayings and stories in order to refresh their memories even before the first Gospel was written. Thus as far as the life and teaching of Jesus are concerned we have an unbroken line of information stretching back to the time of his ministry.

It is of course far more important that we should be able to feel that we can rely on the New Testament, particularly the Gospels, than was the case with the Old Testament. It does not really matter very much whether we have a correct record of what Abraham or Elijah said and did, but it does matter vitally in the case of Jesus. Yet we must be sensible about this. There was no miraculous protection of the New Testament writings any more than of any other ancient documents. Like everything else, the New Testament depends on human memories which can make mistakes. We have to allow for the possibility of misunderstanding and occasional confusion. On the face of it a saying of Jesus which is short and crisp, and which was probably repeated over and over again in the course of Jesus' ministry, like, for example, 'Always treat others as you would like them to treat you' (Matthew 7: 12), is much more likely to be remembered accurately than a single incident seen by a few people only, like the Transfiguration of Jesus (Mark 9: 1–8). We have also to take into account that before the invention of printing, the Gospels were copied by hand for centuries, resulting in inevitable mistakes, missing out a word or a line here, and repeating a word or a line there. Fortunately mistakes of this kind can be and have been largely eliminated by comparing the vast number of manuscript copies of the New Testament originating in different places and at different times.

FACTS AND THEIR MEANING

There is however one major difference between modern historians and biographers and those of biblical times which we must always bear in mind. Both in the Old Testament and in the New Testament the writers are never concerned merely with writing down what we call 'facts', but always much more with the meaning and significance of the events they are describing.

Let us take an example from the Old Testament. In the first book of Kings (16: 21–28) we are told all that the Bible thinks we ought to know about Omri, king of Israel, who reigned in the 9th century B.C. It sums him up in six verses, but goes on to devote six chapters to his son Ahab (1 Kings 16: 29–22: 40). Yet we know from Assyrian inscriptions that Omri was a powerful monarch and successful soldier, whose military prowess made such an impression on the war-loving Assyrians that a hundred and fifty years later they were still calling Israel the land of 'the house of Omri'. His son Ahab was a much less notable figure in world affairs, but he and his queen Jezebel had a profound effect on the religious and social life of Israel. The Bible is much more interested in this than in listing the battle honours of Omri, and so it devotes six verses to Omri but six chapters to Ahab, one of which is solely concerned with the right of a peasant farmer, Naboth, to refuse the king permission to take his vineyard from him and add it to the royal palace gardens which it adjoined (1 Kings 21).

It is this attitude of the biblical writers and their concern for the significance of history, rather than the facts of history, that explains why the great battle of Karkar in 853 B.C. between the Assyrians and a coalition of Palestinian states in which the army of Israel under Ahab played a notable part, and which is fully documented in Assyrian records, is not even mentioned in the Bible.

The same thing is true when we turn to the New Testament. No self-respecting modern biographer would leave out so much detail in writing a life of Jesus as we find when we read the Gospels. We are not told what Jesus looked like, how he spoke and what he wore, or what he was doing for almost thirty years, the 'hidden years', before he began his public ministry. We are not sure how long his ministry lasted, or whether it was largely spent in Galilee with only the last week in Jerusalem, or whether it centred to a much larger extent on the capital. We are not given a day by day chronicle of Jesus' activities, nor anything like a full account of all the things he said. What we do get is a selection of incidents—acts of healing, encounters with the religious authorities, occasional glimpses of his family and his closest friends. Only when we reach Passion Week is there any attempt to give the kind of detailed narrative that we should like to have. This is simply because the Gospel writers were conscious all the time that this was no ordinary life that they were describing, but the words and deeds of one whom they had come to acknowledge as Messiah and Lord. There was no room in such a story for the kind of gossip and tittle tattle that we should expect to find in a life of Winston Churchill or Queen Victoria. Nevertheless, as we shall see, we are given enough information to leave us with a clear impression of the kind of person Jesus was and of the impact he made on those around him.

What we have been looking at so far is roughly the view of the Bible held by modern biblical scholars. The work of biblical experts based on a scientific study of Old and New Testaments over the past century or so has undoubtedly given us a far deeper understanding of the nature of the Bible, of how it came into being, and how we can answer some of the questions that any intelligent reader of the Bible nowadays finds himself asking. When we come to look more closely at the actual contents of the Bible we shall have to raise the larger question of the relevance of the Bible for the twentieth century, but first we must ask a prior question, which is: What is the authority of the Bible in the light of modern scholarship?

Before the upheaval caused last century by the revolutionary discoveries of Darwin and other scientists about the origin of man and the age of rocks, to be followed by new scientific knowledge about the size of the universe, it was generally believed by ordinary churchpeople that the Bible provided an infallible guide as to how the world was created, how life appeared on it, and indeed that the Bible could be relied on to provide all the information we needed to have about geology, biology, astronomy, geography and the history of the ancient world. The battle between the defenders of the Bible and the scientists was long and fierce. But we now know that the scientists were right and the organised Church was wrong; and it was largely through the work of devout biblical scholars that the Church came to see its mistake.

It is now recognised that the Bible cannot be infallible, because it was written by human beings, who can never be infallible. God has revealed the truth about himself and us in the Bible, but he has entrusted his Word to recorders with all the limitations of faulty memories and imperfect understanding. This is no more surprising than that he entrusted the fullest revelation of himself to a village carpenter from Nazareth, or the foundation of his Church to a group of working folk, some of them fishermen. At one time it was believed that the human element in the Bible was ruled out because the writers had simply held the pens, and the Holy Spirit had guided their hands. That would not have been inspiration but something more like magic.

If the authority of the Bible does not depend on its infallibility, can we then say that it depends on its inspiration, that is, that God in some way inspired its writers? This is not very satisfactory either, because we must recognise that God has inspired all the writers of great books, painters of great pictures and composers of great music. He has inspired the writers of the sacred books of all world religions, as well as the writers of Christian classics like *Pilgrim's Progress* and many splendid hymns. We should also have to admit that there is nothing very inspired about the measurements for Solomon's Temple (1 Kings 6–7), the regulations for animal sacrifice in Leviticus, or the command to kill all witches (Exodus 22: 18).

The real authority of the Bible for us today, as it always has been, is that it is the book that tells us about Jesus. Many books have been written about Jesus since his day but the Bible is unique in that it is the original record of his life on earth, his ministry and teaching, his death and resurrection. The Old Testament tells how the way was prepared for his coming, how one people—the Jews—was chosen to be the means of communicating to the world the truth about God and his plan for man's salvation, and how God revealed to the prophets, psalmists and sages of Israel insights which made men ready to receive the full disclosure of the meaning of life and of God's purpose for his creation when he revealed it fully in the person and work of Christ. The rest of the New Testament, after the Gospels, also centres on Jesus, telling of the beginning of the Church which he founded to do his work in the world and of the renewal of society through his spirit.

HOW TO READ THE BIBLE

It is time now to look at the question of how best to read the Bible, and there is no single answer. But however we set about it we must get hold of a modern translation. The language of the Authorised Version of 1611 is magnificent but often obscure, because of the change in the use and meaning of words since Shakespeare's day. Moreover many more ancient manuscripts of both Old and New Testaments have been discovered since then, so that it is possible now to arrive at a translation that is much closer to the original Hebrew and Greek.

When it comes to selecting a modern translation the choice is embarrassing, particularly in the case of the New Testament. The New English Bible, containing Old and New Testament and Apocrypha, was first published in this complete form in 1970 and it is strongly to be recommended as being both accurate and readable. Older people familiar with the Authorised Version miss some of the familiar passages in well-loved words, but for younger people there can be no question but that the New English Bible is the version that will be most helpful. But how do we set about reading it? Some brave souls set out to read the Bible like a novel from beginning to end. This can definitely be said not to be the best way. We may start off well enough with Genesis and some of Exodus, but we are pretty certain to get bogged down in Leviticus. The late Bishop Wilson of Birmingham, who was a prisoner of war in the notorious Changi camp was asked by some of the British prisoners if he thought it would be all right if they used a Bible for cigarette paper. His understanding reply was: "Yes it will be all right. Begin with Leviticus".

A better suggestion is to read a book of the Bible at a sitting, selecting groups of books of different types, say Mark—Philippians—Genesis—Amos; next Luke—Ephesians—Exodus—Isaiah 40–55, and so on. Other people with less time prefer to follow a lectionary, while others again find I.B.R.A. Daily Bible Readings more satisfactory. It is really a matter of what suits us best or what fits in best with what other things we have to do. Whichever method of reading the Bible we use further help can be obtained from simple commentaries. Your minister would be able to advise you on this. It would also be a good idea to begin your course of Bible study by reading a simple introduction to the whole Bible, which would give you a general idea of the Bible and how it fits together. A good book for this purpose is Alice Parmelee's *Guidebook to the Bible* in the popular 'Teach Yourself' series. In the second half of this present short book we shall try to get an impression of the Bible as a whole, necessarily very brief but, I hope, helpful.

PAGEANT, DRAMA OR STORY?

The Bible has been described as a historical pageant, with generation after generation of men and women flitting across its pages, all having to cope with the problems that faced them in their particular times. In this pageant there are moments of peculiar intensity when history acquires a new meaning and events take a new direction. If we think of the Bible in this way we could say that there were three turning points of this kind: the first centring on Moses at the time of the Exodus, the second being the age of the great prophets beginning with Amos, and the third the coming of Christ and his impact on the world. These three periods can be thought of as moments of special illumination, when, as it were, the heavens were opened and men saw for a brief space new truths about God and themselves, after which the world could never be the same again.

Another way of looking at the Bible is to think of it as a dramatic presentation of the Acts of God in history, indeed as a kind of Divine Drama. Those who prefer to view the Bible in this way claim that

the drama divides itself neatly into three acts, with a prologue and an epilogue. The prologue would be the first few chapters of Genesis (1–11), Act I would cover the rest of the Old Testament from Genesis 12 to Malachi, Act II would be the Gospels and Act III the rest of the New Testament, excluding the book of Revelation, which would be the epilogue.

Yet again a third way of looking at the Bible is to think of it not so much as a drama, which tends to suggest that we are simply spectators, but rather as a story—a dramatic one indeed—which begins with the creation of the world and is still going on. This way we are reminded that the story of the Bible is our story. We are all part of it, Christians and non-Christians, men and women of all races, saints and sinners, high and low, rich and poor, wise and foolish.

But whichever way we choose to look at the Bible, we must remember first of all that it is a unity from cover to cover despite all the variety of its style and contents; secondly, that it is a book about action, about the kind of things God does and the kind of things people do. It is a book about life, about the human scene—about war and peace, love and hate, cruelty and kindness, the rise and fall of nations and empires, success and failure, despair and hope. It is about honesty and dishonesty, social corruption and social welfare, about man's quest for a meaning in life, and his aspirations towards something better than he knows, but also about his greed and selfishness which defeat his best intentions.

This is life as we know it and as it has always been. But the Bible shows us the other side too—the power of God working all the time to bring order out of chaos, to promote good instead of evil, to give hope and encouragement, and to provide us with an anchor in the stormy seas that surround us. It shows us how God has spoken to men and women who were ready to listen, and how he has used them to lead others to see more clearly what life is about, the direction we ought to be going, and what lies at the end of our journey. The Bible shows us that life is a pilgrimage whose end is beyond this present world, but that every step we take on this stage of our journey matters. It sees us stumbling and falling, wandering off the way that God wants us to go, burdened with a load of past mistakes, but always being given the chance to start again on the right road.

THE PROBLEM OF RELEVANCE

Let us try then to see the Bible as a connected whole, looking for the main themes and patterns and not worrying too much about detail. This is particularly necessary in the case of the Old Testament, for as the Chinese pastor implied (p. 6) crab shell is pretty indigestible. With the best will in the world it is difficult to find much relevance for today in much of the legislation connected with animal sacrifice, priestly vestments, or kosher food. These matters seem to be so tied up with ancient Jewish practices, from which Christianity has departed, that we can hardly feel that they are of vital concern to us now. The difficulty however is that if, for example, having taken a quick look at the book of Leviticus, and having decided that there is nothing in it for us, we should tend to dismiss the whole book as irrelevant, we should be throwing away at least one injunction which Jesus made the royal law for his followers: Love your neighbour as yourself (Leviticus 19: 18; Mark 12: 31; James 2: 8). And if we simply brush aside all the instructions connected with the Jewish priesthood in the Old Testament, we shall find it difficult to make much sense of the letter to the Hebrews in the New Testament, which is largely concerned with the priesthood of Jesus and in particular with the connection between the Jewish Day of Atonement and Christ's atoning sacrifice (Leviticus 16; Hebrews 9).

Similarly, although by and large the story of the journey of the Israelites through the wilderness at the time of the Exodus seems to have little point for us now, we cannot overlook that it was from the incident of the discovery of manna (Exodus 16) that Jesus drew the sublime parallel of himself as the bread of life (John 6: 30–58). Likewise the melancholy record in I and II Kings of the largely mediocre kings of Israel and Judah, between the spacious days of David and Solomon and the final collapse of the monarchy in 587 B.C., appears to have little of value for us today. But if we were simply to dismiss it all as what Carlyle called 'Hebrew old clothes', we should miss the splendid story of the prophet Micaiah in 1 Kings 22, which tells of a man who insisted on speaking the truth even though it cost him his life.

In taking this bird's eye view of the Bible let us then by all means avoid getting bogged down with detail, but at the same time keep our eyes open for any special insights that come our way even in the most unlikely places. This is what is meant by saying that it is the whole Bible which is God's revelation, and not just the parts that we like best or which seem most revelant in our time. It is in this sense also that we can still call the Bible the Word of God, even although we no longer think of it as infallible in the way Dean Burgon defined it in a sermon in 1861: "Every book of it, every chapter of it, every word of it, every syllable of it (where are we to stop?), every letter of it, is the direct utterance of the Most High". This would make the Almighty guilty among other things of giving his blessing to those who dash children to death against rocks (Psalm 137: 9). Words like these are not words of a God of love but of a man blinded by a lust for vengeance. God still speaks to us in the Bible, not in every word or in every verse, but in the Old and New Testaments as a whole which bring us face to face with Christ.

THE PROLOGUE

Whether we think of the Bible as a pageant, a drama or a story, it begins with what can best be regarded as a prologue, for the first eleven chapters of Genesis are quite different in character from what follows. From Genesis 12 onwards we are dealing with the story of God's choice of Israel, beginning with Abraham, to be a special channel of his revelation of himself and his purpose to mankind. It is therefore history, though there is a large amount of legend too. But the first eleven chapters of Genesis are not historical at all except in the widest sense. There is obviously a universe of which our earth forms part and which must have come into existence somehow and at some time. And as we have seen (pages 16–19), there was a great flood in ancient times in Mesopotamia. But by and large these early chapters of Genesis are best described as parables, or simply as stories. They are there to paint a vivid picture of the marvellous world God created and the purpose he had in mind for it, followed by a series of sketches of the horrible mess men and women have always made of it. The prologue is thus not so much about things that happened long ago but about the way people have always behaved and are still behaving.

ADAM AND EVE

The magnificent first chapter of Genesis is a hymn to the glory of God the Creator. It is not a scientific account of how the world came into being—even the scientists themselves cannot agree on that—nor does it attempt to prove that God exists. The unknown writer knew how wonderfully God had guided the fortunes of the Hebrew people, and he knew the presence of God in his own experience. So he invites us here to believe that the same good God was the power that created all that is, sun, moon, stars, the good earth with all its creatures, and, to crown all, men and women. But unlike the other animals God made men and women 'in his own image', that is, able to make contact with him, to be creative like him. So, as we are told, before there was anything there was God, and God delighted in all that he had made.

When we turn to chapter two it seems at first as if this is the same story told over again. That is, however, not so. It is an older version of the story of the Creation by a different writer, who uses the simple language of folk-lore to teach us some very profound things about ourselves and our relation to God. We are given the good earth and its resources for our use, we are given the companionship of marriage for our delight, but at the same time we are reminded that we are not God. We are under his authority and it is for him and not for us to set the standards of what is good and what is evil. The third chapter shows us that this is exactly what men and women have always refused to accept. The serpent, traditionally cunning and dangerous, is the perfect

symbol of temptation. He plays on man's unwillingness to be subject to any authority beyond his
own. Man insists on running things his own way.
He will brook no interference from God and that
is his downfall.

It need hardly be said that all of this is not about
an actual man, Adam, and his wife Eve. The Hebrew
word Adam means Man, and Eve means Life,
which springs from motherhood. We are being told
in a picturesque way the story of Mr. and Mrs.
Everyman, of men and women as they have always
been. Given freedom to choose obedience to God
or disobedience, our twisted human natures cannot
resist the temptation to please ourselves. Self
becomes our God, and the result as the story
suggests is the breakdown of human relationships
and a barrier between ourselves and God. Thus in

unforgettable symbolism we are shown our human predicament. Made to be sons and daughters of God, men and women through wilful disregard of his authority over their lives, bring disaster upon themselves, ruin the fellowship with one another that they were meant to have, and make it impossible to live in perfect communion with God. But even already, in the symbol of the "tunics of skins" at the end of this third chapter, we are given a hint of God's unwillingness to write off as a failure his experiment of creating man. He still cares for us, despite our sin and folly, and the whole story of the Bible is a development of this theme. Indeed, if we study the first three chapters of Genesis carefully (with a commentary) we shall find that they sum up the essence of the message of the Bible, which is our need for redemption, and point us to its solution in the coming of Christ.

SETH

The remaining chapters of the prologue (Genesis 4–11) intensify the picture of our plight in chapter three. The eldest son of Adam and Eve, Cain, continues and develops his father's self-will. Jealous of his brother, his resentment turns to hate, and hate ends in murder. And remember that the Bible is saying to us: You are all Adam and Eve, and you are all Cains—capable of murder if the occasion arises. Murder, as we know, does not necessarily mean killing with our own hands; it can be done by proxy—by callous indifference to malnutrition, disease and death by violence. Napalm, saturation bombing and other evidences of man's inhumanity to man committed by so-called civilised nations are part of our responsibility. John Donne said: "No man is an island." We are all part of the community of mankind and we are all guilty men—and women. But at the end of the Cain and Abel story in chapter four comes the significant birth of a third son to Adam and Eve—Seth. Again if you look into this (and its sequel in chapter five) you will see that the Bible is introducing a new element into what can only be called man's tragic situation. Seth is made in the image of Adam, and Adam was made in the image of God. In other words, the Bible is saying, you are all Adam, wilful and disobedient, and you are also all Cain, murderers at least by proxy, but you are also all Seth. Seth stands for the God-ward side of Adam, as Cain stands for the brutish side. If you read through the unpromising list of names in chapter five you will see that it ends with Noah, who marks a new beginning in the story of the Bible, and if you turn to Luke 3: 38 you will see that the New Testament traces the ancestry of Jesus back through Noah to Seth. So at this point the prologue is already guiding us to see in Seth the founder of a new type of community in the world which will be focussed on Christ. Whether Seth, or for that matter any other of the characters in the prologue ever existed is not of the slightest importance. The Bible at this stage is not dealing with history but theology. So we need not worry about the fantastic ages of these ancient worthies, not least Methuselah. It was thought that men of old lived longer than we do.

NOAH

Chapters six to nine deal at some length with the story of Noah and the remarkable contents of the Ark. As we have seen (p. 16) this is the Hebrew version of a Babylonian myth. But from the biblical point of view it is included to make the point that despite mankind's utter failure to combat the power of evil in himself and in the world (the mysterious snippet in 6: 1–4 underlines the demonic nature of evil corrupting everything) God is prepared to give mankind a further chance for the sake of one good man. Notice that Noah is not a Christian or even a Jew, but a devout man who lives by the light of his conscience. He stands, we may say, for good men of any religion, and here the Bible asserts their value in the sight of God.

But Noah also establishes another important principle—the power of the one or the few to save the many. This crops up more than once in the Bible before we come to the supreme illustration of it in Christ. The real point of the Noah story for the biblical writer is, however, the covenant in chapter nine. In the story of Cain the Lord put a protective mark on him as a sign of his mercy even to a murderer. Now he establishes a covenant or relationship with Noah on behalf of mankind, by which God promises to maintain man's life on earth, in return for which men must respect their neighbours' right to live. This is the first appearance of the covenant idea which as we shall see runs right through the Bible.

THE TOWER OF BABEL

The last story in the prologue in chapter eleven is that of the legendary Tower of Babel. It is not merely a story about the origin of languages, since we have been told in the previous chapter that different nations already had their own different tongues. It is again a story about man's pride which leads him to disaster. We are shown civilisation on the march. Men are now building cities, but instead of building to the glory of God they want to build to the glory of man. The tower of their temple is to reach to the heavens. Men are to be on a level with God and run the world in their own way, not subject to God's authority. The result of this is that they can no longer co-operate with one another and work together in harmony. The different languages are a symbol of this as St. Luke clearly indicates in the story of Pentecost (Acts 2) when he shows that men began to understand each other again when the power of the spirit of Christ takes hold of them. They speak the common language of Christian love.

The prologue to the Bible has thus shown us what happens when men refuse to acknowledge the authority of God. The world becomes a place of selfish lawlessness. The only law is that of the jungle, and men are kept from destroying each other only by fear of the consequences. But this is not the kind of world that God intended and the rest of the Bible tells of how God intervened to save man from himself and rescue him from the morass into which his selfishness leads him. In the first few verses of

Genesis 12 we are told how one man, Abraham, in the line of succession from Seth (Luke 3: 34 ff.), first responded to God's call and became the founding father of a new community through whom God will lead men back to himself. Through this man and his descendants God will reveal the truth about himself, the purpose of life, and the way men must go if they are to live in harmony with the Creator and with one another.

THE DIVINE DRAMA: ACT 1

From Genesis 12 to the end of the Old Testament, we have what may be called Act 1 of the divine drama. It is the longest of the three acts and it traces the fortunes and misfortunes of the Hebrew people. We are shown their obscure origin as a nomadic tribe under Abraham, who is presented as a man fit to be the father of a people with a unique destiny in the world. Lively stories, vividly told, give us a picture of these early days in Palestine, until in time of famine Abraham's grandson Jacob and his family seek food and refuge in the neighbouring friendly country of Egypt. One of Jacob's sons, Joseph, rises to become Prime Minister of Egypt, and the book of Genesis concludes with the dramatic story of his achievements.

MOSES

But in time the fortunes of the Hebrews suffer a reverse. A new dynasty comes to power in Egypt and Joseph's descendants are no longer welcome. The Hebrews are enslaved and ill-treated and indeed face extermination. At this point, however, a deliverer appears in the person of Moses, one of the outstanding figures of history on any showing. The story is told in the book of Exodus of how this great man led his people, then a rabble of despondent slaves, to what was for them the promised land. The escape from Egypt was never looked on by succeeding generations as something they had achieved by their own efforts. It was through this experience that, under the guidance and inspiration of Moses, the Hebrews first became conscious of their high destiny. The story of the Exodus is embellished with a wealth of legend, illustrating how strongly the Hebrews felt that God had miraculously intervened to turn what seemed to be certain death into the road to new life. From Moses they learned to call God by his distinctive Hebrew name of Yahweh, and to recognise that in a peculiarly intimate way he had made them his people, and they must accept him as their Lord. Abraham had made a covenant with God on behalf of himself and his descendants, but now under Moses the covenant-relationship between Yahweh and Israel becomes more explicit. The Ten Commandments (Exodus 20: 1–17), still to this day a worthy code of behaviour for any people, become the standard for the life of this community—the mark of the people of God.

After the death of Moses, the books of Joshua and Judges tell how the Hebrews had to adjust themselves to a different kind of society as they infiltrated into the land of Canaan. They had been shepherds: now they had to become farmers. They had lived in tents: now they had to live in cities. They had known one god, Yahweh, but now Yahweh had to take his place beside the innumerable gods and godesses of their new homeland. In time he tended to become indistinguishable from the rest, and the Ten Commandments became a casualty. Israel wanted to be like other nations, and indeed with their toughness, born of their desert wanderings, they soon took control of their adopted land. They carved out for themselves a small kingdom, under Saul, which his successor David enlarged, and enjoyed a heyday of prosperity, which was enhanced by the commercial skill of David's son Solomon, who bade fair to turn the people of God into another one of the many little principalities of the Levant, no better and no worse than the rest.

But it was not for this that God had called Abraham, and raised up Moses. It was not part of his plan that his chosen people should become like other nations. And so even in these early days voices were heard recalling Israel to its true role in the world—reminding God's people that they were not meant to be like the rest. Samuel, Nathan, and many other nameless prophets emerged to proclaim to their contemporaries that God had some other purpose in mind for them, and if they failed him they would reap the consequences. Things went from bad to worse after Solomon's reign. The kingdom split into two, and the two books of Kings tell the melancholy history of the decline and fall of Israel under generally mediocre rulers, until finally the divided kingdom of Israel was swallowed up by her more powerful neighbours. We are not left to draw our own conclusions as to how this happened. A running commentary is supplied by the prophets of Israel, a unique series of inspired interpreters of contemporary events such as has never appeared in any other nation, beginning with Amos in the middle of the eighth century B.C., and whose words, preserved for us in the Bible, trace the cause of Israel's downfall not so much to the mighty war-machines of Assyria and Babylon as to the failure of Israel to be the people of God that they were meant to be.

EXILE AND RETURN

We are given a picture by one prophet after another of a country tottering to its doom because of its inner corruption—injustice, extortion, exploitation of the poor, superficiality in religion, sensuality in moral behaviour. You are no people of God, cried the prophets, but an abomination in his sight. So Israel, having turned her back on Yahweh, having forgotten Moses, and flouted the Commandments, was written off as a failure. Those who survived the destruction of their land in 587 B.C. were marched in chains

across the desert to exile in far off Babylon, and in the land of their captors they sat down and wept when they remembered Zion (Psalm 137). But once more the merciful hand of God interposed, and they were taught by three of the greatest of the prophets, Jeremiah, Ezekiel and the writer of Isaiah 40–55, to see their exile as a necessary discipline and a time for renewal. God had not given them up. They would return to their old homeland and they would have another chance to rebuild their common life in accordance with the pattern he had given them.

So indeed it might have worked out. Having learned their lesson, those who returned to Palestine determined to purge their community of the flagrant crimes of the past. Gone was the desire to be a nation like other nations. They pledged themselves to be a small community centred on Jerusalem, governed by religious laws derived from the teaching of the prophets, looking to the Temple as the focus of their obedience to God. But as we can see from the books of Ezra, Nehemiah and Jonah, it was not the broad humanity of the prophets that dominated their lives, nor their task to carry the good news of Israel's God to the Gentiles that filled their thoughts, but a narrow self-centred intolerance of anything and anybody outside the closed circle of their Jewish heritage. The mark of the people of God was to be racial purity, circumcision, kosher food and sabbath observance. So they substituted the sins of the spirit for the sins of the flesh, and failed once again to be a worthy example to the rest of the world of what it meant to be God's chosen people. In this long Act I of the divine drama we are shown that not all the high principles and inspired instruction given through prophets, psalmists and sages can straighten the twist in human nature and overcome the evil tendencies that thwart men's best intentions. Something more than good advice is needed, and that is what Act II of the drama goes on to describe.

THE DIVINE DRAMA: ACT II

It is clear from even the most casual dipping into the Old Testament that the Hebrews were not chosen to be the people of God because they had a flair for religion or more than their share of the virtues. Their record shows them to have had the normal quota of liars, murderers, adulterers, and twisters such as are found in any community. But within the nation from the Exodus onwards, there was a unique succession, beginning with Moses, of men of deep convictions and high principles, the prophets of Israel and their disciples, who saw to it that however indistinguishable the religious and political life of the people was from that of any other Near Eastern country, the faith of Israel, as distinct from its state religion, was kept alive, and the standards of the Ten Commandments were never allowed to be forgotten. It was this faithful minority within the nation which through the centuries brought about reforms in the state religion, took to task kings and statesmen on behalf of the rights of ordinary citizens, and sought by word and action, in season and out of season, to recall the people to the service of God.

This was no easy matter. It was difficult to convince the rank and file of the community that their God Yahweh was concerned about them, when the country seemed to stagger from one disaster to another, and when, instead of receiving some marks of the Lord's favour, things went progressively from bad to worse. They found themselves at the mercy of one great empire after another—a powerless pocket-handkerchief of a community, clinging to a few acres of barren soil among the Judaean hills. Yet, so strong was the conviction of that faithful minority that Yahweh would never utterly forsake his chosen people, that they never lost hope of better things to come. Indeed the blacker the prospects seemed around them the stronger grew their hope. They were certain that one day God would come to the rescue of his people as he had done at the time of the Exodus and again at the Return from Exile.

How this rescue would happen was not clear to them. Sometimes it was thought that political developments in the outside world would bring it about. At other times it seemed that nothing short of a cataclysm could put things right—an end to this corrupt and evil world and the dawning of a new age. Gradually, however, the conviction grew that God would send a Deliverer, a Messiah, who would act on his behalf to vindicate his people in the eyes of the nations, and to prove to the world that the faith of Israel had not been in vain. Some thought in terms of a supernatural Messiah descending from the skies, but most ordinary folk thought that when Messiah came he would come as a liberator of the people from the oppression of the Roman empire, which from 63 B.C. had incorporated the Jews among its subject peoples.

Then about A.D. 30 a handful of undistinguished Jews, led by a fisherman named Peter from Galilee in the north of Palestine, went out into the streets of Jerusalem claiming that Messiah had appeared. Contrary to what everybody expected, he had been Jesus, a carpenter from Nazareth in Galilee, who after conducting a mission of preaching and healing in Galilee, had come to Jerusalem where he had fallen foul of the ecclesiastical authorities, and had been handed over to the Roman government for execution. There had of course been many movements in the country of recent years centring on one or other leader who claimed to be the Messiah, and who collected some followers round him. But Jesus,

asserted Peter and his associates, was someone
different. This was someone who had said things
such as they had never heard before, and exercised
a power over evil which could only come from God,
but above all who had proved himself to be stronger
than death itself, for God had raised him from the
tomb and he had been seen alive by those who now
testified.

JESUS OF NAZARETH

The four gospels, which give us chapter and verse
for the activities of this enigmatic carpenter from
Nazareth, and which we may call the second act of
the divine drama, show us in detail why Peter and
his friends had been drawn into the service of Jesus
and why they had come to acknowledge him as their
Saviour and Lord. It was a gradual awakening of
belief rather than a sudden conversion. That strange
figure John the Baptist, who may be regarded as the
last of the Old Testament prophets, had encouraged
many to look for a speedy coming of the long
expected Messiah, but it seems as if John himself
was never quite sure that Jesus was indeed God's
promised Deliverer. Jesus did not fit in with John's
ideas of what Messiah would be like, any more than
he fitted in with the expectations of the Jewish
church authorities. But Peter and his friends had
lived with Jesus during the years of his Galilean
mission. They had seen him calm men's tortured
minds and heal their tormented bodies. They had
heard from his lips words which no ordinary man

dared utter, and in his presence they felt that somehow they were in the presence of God.

Perhaps the most impressive feature of Jesus' ministry was his authority. When the greatest of the Old Testament prophets had delivered their message they had always regarded themselves as speaking on behalf of God. They prefaced their most trenchant utterances with the words: Thus saith the Lord. But Jesus went further. He dared to call in question the sacred words of Moses himself, setting himself up as a greater authority. Despite what you have been told in the scriptures, said Jesus, I tell you. He avoided using the word Messiah about himself. Yet when he asked his disciples point blank: Who do you say that I am? Peter answered for them all when he replied: You are the Messiah (Mark 8: 29).

But of course Peter shared with the other members of the small group of followers that Jesus had gathered round himself the common ideas of what Messiah would do. This was certainly not what was in Jesus' mind. At his baptism (Matthew 3: 16–17) he had had a vision of God and divine assurance that he was indeed the Messiah. We may guess that in the 'hidden years' Jesus had had a growing awareness that he was not like other men, and no doubt when he left Nazareth and went south to where this strange prophet John the Baptist was drawing the crowds, with his message that Messiah would soon appear, it was to seek a word from God which would clear his mind as to whether he himself might be destined to be the chosen instrument of God's purpose on earth. At his baptism he heard the decisive words and received the power of God's Spirit. From then on he had no doubts, and the story of the Temptation (Matthew 4: 1–11) is a picturesque account of how he dismissed as unworthy the common beliefs as to what Messiah would do. Jesus returned from this inward struggle with his mind made up.

He would take as the pattern of his Messiahship the Servant of God spoken of in the book of Isaiah, who would proclaim the good news of God's love to his people, liberate them from their fears and from the power of evil over their minds and bodies (Luke 4: 16–21 see Isaiah 61: 1–4). So he went back from the Jordan to his own land of Galilee and to a ministry of perhaps three years. He was acclaimed for his healing powers, but his teaching proved too demanding for most of his hearers. The way was too hard—the way of unselfishness and love—and it became clear to Jesus that there would be no massive revival, no widespread change of heart. He therefore concentrated on the small band of his closest followers who had at least glimpsed something of the truth about life and how it should be lived. They would form the nucleus of his new community, they would be the New Israel, fulfilling the task that the old Israel had failed to accomplish.

OPPOSITION

Meanwhile, opposition from the orthodox ecclesiastics mounted. They distrusted this vagrant preacher who played fast and loose with the sacred scriptures, violating the sabbath, reinterpreting the Ten Commandments, ignoring the laws about ritual cleanliness, mixing with the riff-raff of society, "tax gatherers and sinners", worst of all claiming to forgive men their sins. Such a dangerous character must be got rid of, and Jesus faced not only the failure of his mission but his certain death. Yet was not this what the prophet had foretold would happen to the Servant of God—rejection and execution, but also the promise that by his death he would save his people and that beyond his death lay his vindication (Isaiah 53)?

Jesus had to persuade Peter and his other disciples that this was what Messiahship involved and not earthly glory. They found it hard to believe and impossible to understand. Jesus had made up his mind that he must bring matters to a head in the nation's capital Jerusalem, where so many prophets had suffered before, and where blatant corruption in the Temple itself, the heart of Israel's religious life, dishonoured God and made a mockery of Israel's claim to be in any sense still his people. As he entered Jerusalem, Jesus demonstrated by his actions that he now openly claimed to be Messiah by fulfilling the words of Zechariah (9: 9). Then by driving out the hucksters who had turned the Temple into a fairground, thereby lining the pockets of the ecclesiastics, he struck a blow in the name of God against the travesty of religion that the ancient faith of Israel had become.

It was inevitable after this that there could be no alternative to Jesus' trial and execution, unless the authorities had been willing to acknowledge him as Messiah. And so, deserted even by his closest followers, Jesus was crucified under Roman law and buried in a nearby sepulchre. As he hung on the cross, after a momentary cry when he felt himself forsaken by God as well as men, his last words were a prayer for forgiveness for his enemies and a final commitment of his soul to God. Even the Roman centurion presiding over Jesus' execution was moved to exclaim: "Beyond all doubt this man was innocent" (Luke 23: 47).

It was probably an Irishman who said that if the gospels had ended with the crucifixion they would never have been written. Whether it was or not, whoever said it was undoubtedly right. For the gospels were not written by men who believed that they were writing the life story of a great prophet, or handing on to posterity the words of a beloved teacher. Rather they were men who had set themselves the task of recording the good news that at last man's greatest enemy, death, had been defeated by the Resurrection of Jesus. Tallyrand was once asked how to found a new religion. His reply was: Try getting yourself crucified and rising again on the third day. For this fact of the Resurrection was what launched Christianity as a world faith. If Christianity had simply been based on the moral teaching of Jesus, it might have survived for a time as a sect of

The empty tomb

the Jewish Church, comparable to the Essenes of Qumran who have bequeathed us the Dead Sea Scrolls and little else. It would certainly not have become a life-changing movement which swept through the Roman Empire, and since then has won the allegiance of men and women of every race in all corners of the known world.

It has been able to do this because the handful of Jews who on what we call Good Friday were in black despair because they had seen their Messiah tortured and killed, were a few days later on top of the world, because their Master had vanquished death, had risen from the sepulchre where he had been buried, had appeared to them and spoken with them, and was now with them in a deeper sense than he had ever been before. It was with this conviction that a few weeks later they set out to convert the world. An American sceptic devoted two years study to examining all the evidence for the Resurrection, in order to prove that it had never happened. Instead, he reached the conclusion that it was the best attested fact in history.

THE DIVINE DRAMA: ACT III

The Acts of the Apostles, following the gospels begins what we may call the third act of the divine drama. It makes fascinating reading. The author of the book was also the author of the third Gospel, Luke, and he obviously designed Acts as the second part of a two volume work, covering the life and teaching of Jesus and its sequel in the story of the beginning of the Church. Luke makes it plain that he saw the ministry of Jesus continuing in the ministry of his disciples. For a period of about six weeks after the Resurrection, the risen Christ moved among his followers instructing them as to their future programme, enlightening them about many points in his teaching that still puzzled them. Then, when he felt he had convinced a sufficient number that he was in fact still alive, he left them with the promise that he would send his Spirit to be with them wherever they went and to give them the power to carry on the work that he had begun.

On the day of Pentecost, which became our Whitsunday, the disciples experienced a mighty visitation of the Spirit which launched the Church on its mission. Peter, as the chief spokesman, began in Jerusalem a preaching campaign in which he sought to persuade those Jews who would listen that Jesus of Nazareth had been their Messiah, proving from Old Testament scriptures that what their own prophets and psalmists had foretold about God's deliverance of his people had now come true. He called on them to repent of their crime of rejecting their Messiah, inviting them to be baptised as a mark of their incorporation into the new community, assuring them that if they did so they would receive God's forgiveness, and the same power from the Holy Spirit which the disciples themselves had received.

At first the community met together regularly for instruction and prayers, including a simple type of eucharistic celebration, which they called 'breaking bread'. So strong was their sense of fellowship that they shared their possessions with one another with the result that no one was in need. They were in high favour with the ordinary citizens of Jerusalem, partly because they were obviously devout, and regular in their attendance at the Temple, partly because the healing power of the apostles was clearly a gift from God, but perhaps most of all because their lives were such splendid evidence of the reality of their faith. The Jewish religious leaders were less well disposed, however, since they had hoped to put an end to the Jesus-cult by having him put to death. Now it was stronger than ever, but they were dissuaded from further action by counsels of moderation from such an influential person as Gamaliel, a leading Pharisee (Acts 5: 33 ff.).

STEPHEN

Luke does not pretend that even in those halcyon days the life of the young Church was all sweetness and light. There were black sheep in the community, such as Ananias (5: 1–12), and, as numbers increased, dissension arose over the question of fair distribution of poor relief between the native Jerusalem Jewish Christians and those Jewish Christians who had lived abroad and had then settled in Jerusalem. It is clear from chapter six that there was more to it than a quarrel over poor relief. The more liberal-minded Jewish Christians from overseas wanted a bigger say in the Church, and so it was agreed that seven of them should be appointed, ostensibly to assist the apostles. It soon transpired that one of these, Stephen, was concerned with more than social welfare. Stephen was a radical who was, as far as we can judge, the first Christian to recognise that Judaism and Christianity would not mix. Like all Christian Jews he was proud of his Old Testament heritage, the legacy of the prophets and psalmists of Israel. But he was highly critical of the current obsession with Jewish ecclesiastical practice, whereby the sacred soil of the holy land had acquired almost supernatural qualities, the cult of the Temple had become next-door to idolatrous, and circumcision was treated as a fetish. He was arrested for preaching subversive doctrines and stoned to death by an outraged mob.

His death marked a new stage in the spread of the gospel. Persecution broke out, and those who sympathised with Stephen's radical views were driven from their homes in Jerusalem and scattered through the countryside. But wherever they went they preached the gospel. From then on the story of the Church is the story of how one barrier after another was broken down, and Jewish prejudices, which sought to keep Jews apart from the rest of the world, were overcome by Christian Jews sharing Stephen's liberal outlook—which was of course a practical expression of Jesus' own attitude. It was the power of his Spirit at work.

PAUL

So the gospel was preached to the Samaritans, traditionally hated by all good Jews, and a devout African official, a eunuch, who for that reason was not eligible to become a member of the old people of God, was baptised and welcomed into the community of the New Israel.

The most dramatic development in the progress of the Church was the conversion of Saul of Tarsus, a brilliant rabbi who had supported the murder of Stephen, and was bent on eradicating completely the mischievous Christian heresy which threatened to destroy the God-given laws and customs of the Jewish people. On the road to Damascus he came face to face with the risen Christ, and knew that the Jesus whose followers he had so venomously persecuted was no deluded crank but indeed God's Messiah. From then on for the rest of his life Paul was utterly committed to Christ and became his tireless advocate. His strongest supporter in this was Peter, who had been moved by unmistakably divine prompting to baptise Cornelius, a Roman centurion (Acts 10), and this action by the chief apostle gave official approval to the Gentile mission.

The remainder of the Book of Acts is taken up largely with the expansion of the Church and the spread of Christianity among the Gentiles. It is primarily the story of Paul himself, an indefatigable missionary, pushing out the frontiers of the Church throughout the Mediterranean world until it reached the capital of the Empire, Rome itself. Paul did not do this singlehanded. He had many assistants, whom we can read about in Acts, and there were even more anonymous Jewish Christian merchants and traders with their families who spread the gospel as they went about their business.

The rest of Act III of the divine drama, which occupies the remainder of the New Testament, consists mainly of letters from Paul and other missionaries to the young Christian churches which had been founded in the pagan world. From them we learn of the growing pains and teething troubles of the early Church, of opposition and persecution, and disputes within the congregations, as they sought to cope with life in the cosmopolitan cities, and tried to adjust what was essentially a Jewish faith to the complex problems of the Gentile world.

In this process the master mind was that of Paul himself, who not only laid the foundations of the Church as we know it today, but also in his letters put into words his own profound understanding of the significance of Jesus for people in any age and in any society.

The Divine Drama does not end with the New Testament. It still goes on wherever men and women moved by the spirit of Christ seek to bring our common life more into harmony with the will of God. All who have committed their lives to Christ have still a role to play in this drama, when, in their homes or in their jobs or in the wider service of the community, they act, in Paul's words, as 'Christ's ambassadors' (2 Corinthians 5: 20). Whenever we get discouraged in this task we may turn to the Book of Revelation, which may be regarded as the Epilogue to the Divine Drama, where, in symbolic language of breath-taking magnificence, we are shown the ultimate victory of God and the defeat of evil, when Christ the Redeemer gathers his people into the unimaginable splendour of the presence of God.

THE BIBLE AND OURSELVES

We began by claiming that the Bible is like no other book in the world. Whether this is true or not is a question that can only be answered by each one of us for himself, for the Bible presents us all with an invitation and a challenge. It asks us to take a good long look at ourselves and the world we live in. We know, if we are honest with ourselves, what a mixture we are. In our best moments we want to be good fathers and mothers, good sons and daughters, good members of our community. But so often our own selfishness defeats us. Like Adam and Eve we prefer to please ourselves, rather than acknowledge that we are all subject to an authority beyond ourselves, the authority of God.

The Bible invites us to believe that the only way we can live at peace with ourselves and with the world around us is to acknowledge that we are doomed to frustration and failure when we tell ourselves that "we know best". We are in fact poor shiftless mortals who have the greatest difficulty in keeping our feet in a bewildering and changing world. The Bible offers us an anchor, in the belief that the whole world and our own lives are in the hands of a God who cares for us and wants us to be his sons and daughters. It tells us that he wants us to have the full life that Jesus promised, and that we can only have that if we commit our lives to him. Jesus did not come merely to leave us his example to follow but he is still with us as a present power in our lives, constantly calling us to penitence for our failures and assuring us of God's forgiveness.

Yet the Bible also presents us with a challenge. The prophets of Israel, and Jesus himself, had no doubt that belief in God means involvement in the affairs of the world. The Christian life is not merely a matter of prayer and reading the Bible. We are called to play our part and take our share in the more difficult role of helping towards the renewal of the life of society. Let us not exaggerate. Most of us are not likely to become Prime Ministers, captains of industry, or even Members of Parliament. Our influence as Christians is much more likely to be confined to smaller fields. Some of you may be given the chance of changing the pattern of your Trade Union, your professional association, your local congregation, to bring them more into line with what you believe Christ intended. But for the majority of us it will be a matter of sowing seed, like the sower in Jesus' parable (Mark 4). Some seed will fall on stony ground and some among thistles, but the odd word of friendliness, sympathy, counsel and guidance which falls on good ground will, as Jesus said, bear fruit "even a hundredfold". And remember, again as Jesus has shown us, it is not just words that count, but actions. Who can estimate the contribution of a good mother or father, a good son or daughter, a good neighbour, a good citizen, to the redemption of God's world?